2019 | HORSE RIDING IN EVER

INTRODUCT

Hello fellow Equestrian Adventuresses!

Welcome to the Horse Riding in Every Country Catalog for 2019/2020.

We have worked hard to dig deep and find horse trail riding stables, polo clubs and equestrian centers around the world for you to book your next horse vacation, seek volunteer / working positions, go on adventures with and more!

We will be updating this catalog every year so please make sure you have downloaded the most recent edition found on our website: www.equestrianadventuresses.com

This catalog was designed as an easy directory, with clickable links to all the listings in each country.

If you are the owner of a riding stable or holiday destination and are not on this list and would like to be featured in next years catalog please contact us at www.equestrianadventuresses.com

If you book a riding holiday or use any of the stables in this directory, please share your feedback, photos and stories with us! You may email us on our website or join our Facebook Group - Equestrian Adventuresses to let other adventuresses know that you enjoyed your experience!

Happy Trails!
Krystal Kelly
Equestrian Adventuresses Founder

2019 | HORSE RIDING IN EVERY COUNTRY

DISCLAIMER

Although we did our best to include relevant horse riding stables which are active, it is simply impossible for us to physically visit each and every stables on this list to verify them.

Please use caution when booking any horse riding holiday without doing the proper research and vetting of the people, horse care and accommodations.

In the catalog you will be given the website link of each stables in each country (or a facebook page link). It is YOUR RESPONSIBILITY to look at their site's thoroughly, check the reviews, and post in our Facebook Group: Equestrian Adventuresses if you are looking to see other adventuresses stories and photos and reviews of the destination your interested to visit.

Here is a COUPON to our Women's Travel Safety Course if you have any concerns and would like to learn some tactics about solo women travel.

# VERIFIED BADGE

The Verified Badge is our promise to you that the stables holding this badge have met our quality check and standards.

The biggest, most important factor when verifying a place is the **welfare of the horses.** If they have happy, healthy horses and are who they say they are (and we've seen it with out own eyes!) then they will receive the verified badge.

If you're unsure, are a first-timer or looking for an adventure which has been done by our team and we can recommend, then look out for the Verified badge!

We DO NOT take commissions for trips we attend. This ensures we remain UNBIASED and fair when deciding to verify and recommend a place. Not all worthy stables have been verified simply because of the logistics behind trying to verify 500 stables around the world. Use your judgement and happy travels!

EQUESTRIAN ADVENTURESSES

2019 | HORSE RIDING IN EVERY COUNTRY

INDEX

A
AFGHANISTAN | PAGE 6
ALBANIA | PAGE 6
ALGERIA | PAGE 6
ANDORRA | PAGE 7
ANTIGUA AND BARBUDA | PAGE 7
ARGENTINA | PAGE 7
ARMENIA | PAGE 8
AUSTRALIA | PAGE 8
AUSTRIA | PAGE 9
AZERBAIJAN | PAGE 9

B
BAHAMAS | PAGE 9
BAHRAIN | PAGE 10
BANGLADESH | PAGE 10
BARBADOS | PAGE 10
BELARUS | PAGE 10
BELGIUM | PAGE 11
BELIZE | PAGE 12
BENIN | PAGE 12
BHUTAN | PAGE 12
BOLIVIA | PAGE 13
BOSNIA AND HERZEGOVINA | PAGE 13
BOTSWANA | PAGE 14
BRAZIL | PAGE 15
BRUNEI | PAGE 16
BULGARIA | PAGE 16
BURKINA FASO | PAGE 16
BURUNDI | PAGE 16

C
CABO VERDE | PAGE 16
CAMBODIA | PAGE 17
CAMEROON | PAGE 17
CANADA | PAGE 17
CHILE | PAGE 18
CHINA | PAGE 19
COLOMBIA | PAGE 19
COSTA RICA | PAGE 20
COTE D'IVOIRE | PAGE 21
CROATIA | PAGE 21
CUBA | PAGE 22
CYPRUS | PAGE 22
CZECH REPUBLIC | PAGE 22

D
DENMARK AND GREENLAND | PAGE 23
DOMINICA | PAGE 24
DRC CONGO | PAGE 24

E
ECUADOR | PAGE 24
EGYPT | PAGE 25
ESTONIA | PAGE 26
ETHIOPIA | PAGE 26

F
FIJI | PAGE 26
FINLAND | PAGE 26
FRANCE | PAGE 27

G
GAMBIA | PAGE 27
GEORGIA | PAGE 27

EQUESTRIAN ADVENTURESSES
PAGE 3

2019 | HORSE RIDING IN EVERY COUNTRY

INDEX

G
GERMANY | PAGE 29
GHANA | PAGE 30
GREECE | PAGE 30
GUATEMALA | PAGE 31

H
HONDURAS | PAGE 31
HONG KONG | PAGE 31
HUNGARY | PAGE 31

I
ICELAND | PAGE 32
INDIA | PAGE 32
INDONESIA | PAGE 34
IRAN | PAGE 34
IRAQ | PAGE 34
IRELAND | PAGE 34
ISRAEL | PAGE 35
ITALY | PAGE 36

J
JAMAICA | PAGE 36
JAPAN | PAGE 36
JORDAN | PAGE 37

K
KAZAKHSTAN | PAGE 38
KENYA | PAGE 39
KUWAIT | PAGE 41
KYRGYZSTAN | PAGE 41

L
LATVIA | PAGE 42
LEBANON | PAGE 42

LESOTHO | PAGE 42
LIBERIA | PAGE 42
LIBYA | PAGE 42
LIECHTENSTEIN | PAGE 43

M
MADAGASCAR | PAGE 43
MALAWI | PAGE 43
MALAYSIA | PAGE 43
MALTA | PAGE 43
MAURITIUS | PAGE 44
MEXICO | PAGE 44
MOLDOVA | PAGE 45
MONGOLIA | PAGE 45
MONTENEGRO | PAGE 46
MOROCCO | PAGE 46
MOZAMBIQUE | PAGE 48
MYANMAR | PAGE 48

N
NAMIBIA | PAGE 49
NEPAL | PAGE 49
NETHERLANDS | PAGE 50
NEW ZEALAND | PAGE 50
NICARAGUA | PAGE 50
NIGER | PAGE 51
NIGERIA | PAGE 51
NORWAY | PAGE 51

O
OMAN | PAGE 51

P
PANAMA | PAGE 51

EQUESTRIAN ADVENTURESSES
PAGE 4

2019 | HORSE RIDING IN EVERY COUNTRY

INDEX

P
PAPUA NEW GUINEA | PAGE 51
PARAGUAY | PAGE 52
PERU | PAGE 52
PHILIPPINES | PAGE 53
POLAND | PAGE 53
PORTUGAL | PAGE 53

Q
QATAR | PAGE 53

R
REPUBLIC OF KOREA | PAGE 54
ROMANIA | PAGE 54
RUSSIA | PAGE 55
RWANDA | PAGE 55

S
SAN MARINO | PAGE 55
SAUDI ARABIA | PAGE 55
SENEGAL | PAGE 55
SERBIA | PAGE 56
SEYCHELLES | PAGE 56
SINGAPORE | PAGE 56
SLOVAKIA | PAGE 56
SLOVENIA | PAGE 56
SOUTH AFRICA | PAGE 57
SPAIN | PAGE 60
SRI LANKA | PAGE 61
ST. KITTS & NEVIS | PAGE 61
ST. LUCIA | PAGE 61

ST. VINCENT & GRENADINES | PAGE 62
SURINAME | PAGE 62
SWAZILAND | PAGE 62
SWEDEN | PAGE 62
SWITZERLAND | PAGE 63

T
THAILAND | PAGE 63
THE REPUBLIC OF NORTH MACEDONIA | PAGE 63
TRINIDAD & TOBAGO | PAGE 65
TUNISIA | PAGE 65
TURKEY | PAGE 65
TURKMENISTAN | PAGE 65
TURKS & CAICOS | PAGE 66

U
UGANDA | PAGE 66
UKRAINE | PAGE 66
UNITED ARAB EMIRATES | PAGE 66
UNITED KINGDOM | PAGE 67
UNITED REPUBLIC OF TANZANIA | PAGE 68
UNITED STATES | PAGE 69

V
VANUATU | PAGE 70
VENEZUELA | PAGE 70
VIETNAM | PAGE 70

Z
ZAMBIA | PAGE 70
ZIMBABWE | PAGE 71

EQUESTRIAN ADVENTURESSES
PAGE 5

2019 | HORSE RIDING IN EVERY COUNTRY

AFGHANISTAN

Silk Road Afghanistan | www.silkroadafghanistan.com

ALBANIA

Illyrian Trail

A time travel trail. Ancient Illyrian ruins, medieval villages, fairytale-like stone bridges over mountain rivers, churches and monasteries, but also traces of Albania's communist past.

http://dirtyhooves.com
Facebook: https://fb.com/dirtyhooves

War Trail

Follow an ancient army route, cross the mountains and reach the shores of the Ionian Sea. See forgotten fortresses in the wild, sometimes accompanied by 20th century bunkers. For experienced riders.

http://dirtyhooves.com
Facebook: https://fb.com/dirtyhooves

Caravan Horse Riding | info@horseridingalbania.com

ALGERIA

Club Hippique De Mostaganem | www.facebook.com/Club-Hippique-De-Mostaganem-29405397716/

EQUESTRIAN ADVENTURESSES

2019 | HORSE RIDING IN EVERY COUNTRY

ALGERIA (CONTINUED)

Haras Hocine El Mansour | www.haras-hm.com

ANDORRA

Equi Libre | www.equi-libre.fr/site/

Hipica Aldosa | www.hipica-aldosa.com/en

ANTIGUA AND BARBUDA

Antigua Equestrian Springhill Riding Club | www.antiguaequestrian.com

ARGENTINA

Estancia Los Potreros

A working family estancia offering a taste of authentic Argentine life. A riding experience that includes over 100 horses, fabulous trail riding, polo, and cattle work.

www.estancialospotreros.com
bookings@estancialospotreros.com

Ampascachi | www.ampascachi.com

Estancia Don Joaquin | www.estanciadonjoaquin.com.ar

2019 | HORSE RIDING IN EVERY COUNTRY

ARGENTINA (CONTINUED)

La Tarde Polo | www.latardepolo.com

Palo Alto Polo | www.paloaltopolo.com

Argentina Polo Day | www.argentinapoloday.com.ar

ARMENIA

Caucasus Journeys | www.caucasusjourneys.com

AUSTRALIA

Bogong Horseback Adventures | www.bogonghorsebackadventures.weebly.com

Centennial Glen Stables | www.centennialglenstables.com

Cowboy Up Trail Riding | www.cowboyup.com.au

Cradle Adventures | www.cradleadventures.com.au

Diggers Rest Station | www.diggersreststation.com.au

Equathon | www.equathon.com

Hepburn Lagoon Rides | www.hepburnlagoonrides.com.au

2019 | HORSE RIDING IN EVERY COUNTRY

AUSTRALIA (CONTINUED)

Rainbow Beach Ride | www.rbhr.com.au

Southern Cross Horse Treks

Adventure Tours through endless Eucalyptus forests, Rainforest, Farmland and Pacific Ocean gallops on forward Arabian horses, small groups, only experienced riders

www.horsetreks.com.au
info@horsetreks.com.au

Thredbo Valley Horse Riding | www.thredbovalleyhorseriding.com

AUSTRIA

Edelweiss Gurgel | www.edelweiss-gurgl.com/en/hotel/riding-stables

Pferdehof Koaserminerl | www.pferdehof-koaserminerl.at/horseback_riding.html

Wiesenhof Hotel | www.wiesenhof.at/en/lake-achensee/horse-riding-austria/61-0.html

AZERBAIJAN

Caucasus Journeys | www.caucasusjourneys.com

Elite Horse Polo Club | www.facebook.com/elitehorseclub/

BAHAMAS

Happy Trails Stables | www.ridingbahamas.com

BAHAMAS (CONTINUED)

Pinetree (Freeport) Stables | www.pinetree-stables.com

BAHRAIN

Dilmun Club | www.dilmun-club.com/dilmun-riding-stables/

Shakhoora Riding Centre | www.shakhooraridingcentre.com

Twin Palms Riding Centre | www.twinpalmsridingcentre.com

BANGLADESH

Horseback riding school Bangladesh | www.facebook.com/equine.business/

BARBADOS

Apes Hill Polo | www.apeshillpolo.com

Ocean Echo Stables | www.barbadoshorseriding.com

Sandy Turf Riding Stables | www.facebook.com/pages/Sandy-Turf-Stables-Barbados

BELARUS

Agrohutor | www.agrohutor.jimdo.com

Koni | www.koni.yadro.by

Spur | www.spur.by

2019 | HORSE RIDING IN EVERY COUNTRY

BELARUS (CONTINUED)

Mustang Club | www.mustang-club.by

BELGIUM

Horse Trail Riding | www.horsetrailriding.be

Hepscheid Long Ear Trails | www.hepscheidlongeartrails.be

Western Trail Ranch | www.ranch.be/pages/nl/de-ranch.php

Franciscushof | www.franciscushof.be

EQUESTRIAN ADVENTURESSES

2019 | HORSE RIDING IN EVERY COUNTRY

BELIZE

Banana Bank | www.bananabank.com

Hanna Stables | www.hannastables.com/horseback-rides/

Mountain Equestrian Trails - MET Outfitters

Ride to waterfalls, jungle river caves and dry caves hidden in protected areas. Challenging mountainous terrain. Exp riders can expect fast canters

www.metbelize.com
metbelize@pobox.com

Outback Trails | www.outbacktrails.com

BENIN

Cotonou | www.cotonou.ffe.com

BHUTAN

Krys Kolumbus Travel

12 Days Riding and Cultural Tour - June 1-12, 2019 Small Group, All-Inclusive. English speaking guides, ride the Himalayas to monasteries. Tiger's Nest Temple finale!

www.kryskolumbustravel.com
krystalkelly009@yahoo.com

 Wind Horse Tours | www.windhorsetours.com

EQUESTRIAN ADVENTURESSES

BOLIVIA

Sucre Horseback riding | www.facebook.com/horsebackridingsucre/

Tupiza Tours | www.tupizatours.com

BOSNIA AND HERZEGOVINA

Djecavjetra | www.djecavjetra.ba

Horse Riding Zadar | www.horseridingzadar.com

KK Hidalgo | www.kkhidalgo.com/en/horseback-riding-lessons-sarajevo/

Pegasos | www.jahanje.ba

2019 | HORSE RIDING IN EVERY COUNTRY

BOTSWANA

Okavango Delta Mobile Camping Safari

Africa's Eden! No vehicles. Environmentally-friendly safari. Enjoy exciting riding & spectacular game viewing, without worrying about your carbon footprint. Private, personalized camp out in the bush.

https://africanhorsesafaris.com
isabel@africanhorsesafaris.com

Botswana's Tuli Safari Trail

Exciting ride through the Limpopo area, famous for elephants. Stay in luxury tented camps & 2 nights sleeping in a boma under the stars. True African wilderness. Fast, fun riding w/ game & jumping logs if you wish!

https://africanhorsesafaris.com
isabel@africanhorsesafaris.com

Kalahari and Makgadikgadi Salt Pans Ride

Prepare to be blown away! Encounter plains, barren salt pans (perfect for galloping) & flora & fauna. See Wildebeest, zebra, elephant, meerkats & more. During migration there are zebra & wildebeest for miles.

https://africanhorsesafaris.com
isabel@africanhorsesafaris.com

EQUESTRIAN ADVENTURESSES

2019 | HORSE RIDING IN EVERY COUNTRY

BOTSWANA (CONTINUED)

Okavango Delta Horse Safari: Macatoo Camp

Vast, untouched landscapes filled w/ game. Exciting riding w/ many water canters. Lodge-based & thrilling rides. Luxury tented camp has private veranda over-looking the flood plains. Non-rider's can join!

https://africanhorsesafaris.com
isabel@africanhorsesafaris.com

South Africa + Botswana Combo Safari

Iconic Africa - canter across open landscapes, stay at bushcamps, search for wildlife. Sundowners, 4 nights in S.A w/ giraffe, zebra and antelopes. Botswana 3 nights - luxury tents, elephants & more!

https://africanhorsesafaris.com
isabel@africanhorsesafaris.com

African Horseback | www.africanhorseback.com

Okavango Delta Explorations | www.okavangodelta.com/tours-safaris/african-horseback-safaris/

Ride Botswana | www.ridebotswana.com

BRAZIL

Riding Brazil | www.ridingbrazil.com

BRUNEI

Royal Brunei Polo Club | www.facebook.com/Royal-Brunei-Polo-and-Riding-Club-134920946518785/

Brunei Bay | www.bruneibay.net/the_royal_experience/equestrianpark.html

BEQ Equestrian Centre | www.facebook.com/Beq-Equestrian-Centre-Sdn-Bhd-246722882021360/

BULGARIA

Horse Riding Bulgaria | www.horseridingbulgaria.com

Horse Riding with Butch | www.horse-riding-bg.com/home/

BURKINA FASO

Faso Du Cheval | www.fasoducheval.wordpress.com

BURUNDI

Cercle Hippique | www.facebook.com/pages/category/Recreation-Center/Cercle-hippique-de-Bujumbura-822988564473627/

Aapkasafar | www.aapkasafar.com/burundi-tours/horse-riding.html

CABO VERDE

Santa Marilha Horse Excursions | www.horseexcursionsal.com

2019 | HORSE RIDING IN EVERY COUNTRY

CAMBODIA

Horseback Cambodia - Liberty Ranch | www.horsebackcambodia.com

The Happy Ranch | www.thehappyranch.com

CAMEROON

Dilmun Club | www.facebook.com/clubsaintgeorges/

Saddle Hill Ranch | www.facebook.com/SaddleHillRanch/

CANADA

Alpine Stables | www.alpinestables.com

Banff Trail Riders | www.horseback.com

Boundary Ranch | www.boundaryranch.com

Broken Trail Ranch | www.brokenrailranch.com/contacthours.html

Flying U Ranch | www.flyingu.com

Icelandic Horse World

5-day riding packages through forests and striking views of the North Okanagan, BC, Canada. Complete with wine tour!

www.icelandichorseworld.com/the-facilities.cfm
contact@icelandichorseworld.com

EQUESTRIAN ADVENTURESSES

2019 | HORSE RIDING IN EVERY COUNTRY

CANADA (CONTINUED)

Horse Play Niagara | www.horseplayniagara.com

Leghorn Ranch | www.vancouverhorsebackriding.com

Trail Riders Canadian Rockies | www.trailridevacations.com

CHILE

Antilco | www.antilco.com

Cabalgata santiago | www.cabalgatasantiago.com

Campesano | www.campesano.com

Chile-Horseriding

Experience the Andes on horseback and change our semi-wild horses to/from the high summer pastures!
> 30 years experience!

www.chile-horseriding.com
info@chile-horseriding.com

Chile Off Track | www.chileofftrack.com

Horse Riding Chile | www.horseridingchile.com

Le Peninsula | www.estanciaspatagonia.com

EQUESTRIAN ADVENTURESSES

2019 | HORSE RIDING IN EVERY COUNTRY

CHINA

Equuleus | www.equriding.com

Goldin Metropolitan Hotel & Polo Club | www.goldinmetropolitanhotel.com

Langmusi Tibetan Horse Trekking | www.langmusi.net

Tibetan Barley Inn | www.tibetanbarley.com/horsetrekking

COLOMBIA

Aventur Eco Tours | www.aventurecotours.com

Cabalgatas El Carmelo | www.cabalgataselcarmelo.com

Cabalgatas San Pablo Talento | www.cabalgatassanpablosalento.com

Horse Shoe Columbia | www.horseshoe-colombia.com

Riding Columbia | www.ridingcolombia.com/en

Valle Verde Horse Riding | www.valleverdehorseriding.com

JOIN THE COMMUNITY

facebook.com/groups/equestrianadventuresses

EQUESTRIAN ADVENTURESSES
PAGE 19

2019 | HORSE RIDING IN EVERY COUNTRY

FOLLOW US & SHARE YOUR PHOTOS
@equestrianadventuresses

COSTA RICA

Barking Horse Farm | www.barkinghorsefarm.com

Caribehorse | www.caribehorse.com

Costa Rica Equestrian Vacation | www.costaricaequestrianvacation.com

CR Beach Barn | www.crbeachbarn.com

Establo San Rafael | www.establosanrafael.com

Finca Caballo Loco | www.fincacaballoloco.com

Hacienda Milbellezas | www.haciendamilbellezas.com

Horse Jungle | www.horsejungle.com

Horse Ride Costa Rica | www.horseridecostarica.com

Horse Trek Monte Verde | www.horsetrekmonteverde.com

Playa Chiquita Riding Adventures | www.playachiquitaridingadventures.com

Rancho Tropical | www.ranchotropical.com

2019 | HORSE RIDING IN EVERY COUNTRY

COSTA RICA (CONTINUED)

Smiling Monte Verde | www.horseback-riding-tour.com

The Riding Adventure | www.theridingadventure.com

Tokpela Costa Rica | www.tokpelacostarica.com

COTE D'IVOIRE

Club Saint Michel | www.facebook.com/Club-Saint-Michel-197339486949755/

Horse Academy De Cote Divoire | www.facebook.com

Poney Club Golf | www.facebook.com/poneyclubgolf/

CROATIA

Equestrian Club Split

Splendid landscape and great horses-that's what awaits you on our trails in Dalmatia and Plitvice.

http://www.equestrianclubsplit.com
info@equestrianclubsplit.com

Kojankoral | www.kojankoral.com/en/

Linden Retreat | www.lindenretreat.com/activities/horse-riding-croatia/

2019 | HORSE RIDING IN EVERY COUNTRY

CROATIA (CONTINUED)

Liska Adventure Riding | www.liska-adventure-riding.business.site

Ranch Chivas | www.ranch-chivas.com

Ranch Istra Star | www.istrastar.com/hr/Default.aspx

CUBA

Rancho El Dajao | www.facebook.com/RanchoElDajao

CYPRUS

Aphrodite Hills Riding Club | www.aphroditehillsridingclub.com

Armageti | www.paphosec.com

Georges Ranch | www.georgesranchcyprus.com

Horse Riding Paphos | www.horseridingpaphos.com

Ride In Cyprus | www.rideincyprus.com

CZECH REPUBLIC

Favory | www.favory.cz

Giant Mountains | www.giant-mountains.info/sport/horse-riding.html

2019 | HORSE RIDING IN EVERY COUNTRY

CZECH REPUBLIC (CONTINUED)

Hospodarskydvur | www.hospodarskydvur.cz

Jkslupenec | www.jk-slupenec.cz/1/en/normal/home/

KONĚ ŘÁSNÁ | www.konerasna.cz

Konevondrov | www.konevondrov.cz

Ludvikovcz | www.ludvikovcz.com

DENMARK

Copenhagen Horseback Riding | www.copenhagen-horsebackriding.com/

Copenhagen Polo Club | www.cphpolo.com/polo-course/

Saga Heste | www.sagaheste.com/

GREENLAND

Riding Greenland - Inneruulalik Sheep-Farm

Ride next to icebergs! 8 Days package w/ 5 days riding - all included. July-August. Group size 2-6 persons, Icelandic horses, experienced riders only.

www.riding-greenland.com
inneruulalik@gmail.com

DOMINICA

Brandy Manor Riding Center | www.brandymanor.wixsite.com/riding-center

Rain Forest Riding | www.rainforestriding.com

DOMINICAN REPUBLIC

Horseplay Punta Cana | www.horseplaypuntacana.com/

Rancho Lorilar | www.rancholorilar1.com/

Rudy's Rancho | www.rudysrancho.com/

DEMOCRATIC REPUBLIC CONGO

Cercle Hippique De Lubumbashi | www.facebook.com/Cercle-Hippique-De-Lubumbashi

CHK Kinshasa | www.chk-kinshasa.com

ECUADOR

Centro Ecuestre Bella Vista | www.centroecuestrebellavista.com/

Green Horse Ranch | www.greenhorseranch.zohosites.com/

Ride Andes | www.rideandes.com

2019 | HORSE RIDING IN EVERY COUNTRY

EGYPT

Luxor and Makadi Bay Ride

Home of the ancient Thebes, thrilling riding on stunning Arab horses, take a trip along the Nile to witness true Arabian village life. Swim with horses & dolphins!

https://africanhorsesafaris.com
isabel@africanhorsesafaris.com

Desert Wind Farm | www.facebook.com/desertwindfarm/

Ride Egypt

Welcome to the land of mystery and allure: Egypt! Multi award winning British brand specialising in authentic riding holidays in Cairo, Luxor & the Red Sea.

http://www.rideegypt.com
info@rideegypt.com

Sharm Horses

Experience the thrilling Arab/Anglo Arab horses - calm, patient & ready to gallop "like the wind!" European mangmnt, friendly & prof staff. Ride in the desert or by the Red Sea all year round. Exp. riders ONLY

www.sharmhorses.com
info@sharmhorses.com

EQUESTRIAN ADVENTURESSES
PAGE 25

ESTONIA

Kuusekannu Riding Farm | www.kuusekannuratsatalu.ee

Xperience by Horse | www.xperiencebyhorse.com/

ETHIOPIA

Beka Ferda Ranch | www.bekaferdaranch.com/

FIJI

Maui Bay Horse Riding Adventure |
www.facebook.com/coralcoasthorseridingadventurcoralcoasthorseriding/

FINLAND

Lapin Saaga Icelandic Horse Stable | www.lapinsaaga.fi

Ride North | www.ridenorth.fi/short.html

2019 | HORSE RIDING IN EVERY COUNTRY

FRANCE

Domaine Equestre des Bastides | www.domaine-equestre-des-bastides.fr/index.php/fr

Ferme de Fonluc | www.fonluc.com/

Touraine Cheval | www.tourainecheval.com/index.html

GAMBIA

Ndungu Kebbe Eco-Lodge & Horse Centre

Unspoilt eco tourist destination. Peaceful, lovely rides to the sea & along old trails past fields of nuts and cous cous. Flora, fauna, birds & wildlife await!
www.ndungukebbe.com
Sister site: http://www.kotuhorses.mozello.com
marysa@ndungukebbe.com

GEORGIA

Greater Caucasus

A magical land of majestic mountains, towers made of stone, home to shepherds and their brave horses. Untouched nature of the Greater Caucasus, amazing culture and famous Georgian hospitality.

www.dirtyhooves.com
ride@dirtyhooves.com

EQUESTRIAN ADVENTURESSES

2019 | HORSE RIDING IN EVERY COUNTRY

DIRTY HOOVES

TRUE HORSEBACK ADVENTURES
RIDE WITH US

ALBANIA | GEORGIA | HUNGARY | KYRGYZSTAN | MOROCCO | PERU | ROMANIA | UKRAINE

DIRTYHOOVES.COM   FB.COM/DIRTYHOOVES

EQUESTRIAN ADVENTURESSES
PAGE 28

2019 | HORSE RIDING IN EVERY COUNTRY

GEORGIA (CONTINUED)

Vashlovani National Park

An amazing safari through the Georgian savanna roamed by wild animals and local shepherds. A week of riding in one of the Georgia's natural wonders - the Vashlovani National Park and Nature Reserve.

www.dirtyhooves.com
ride@dirtyhooves.com

Eat Life | www.wyprawygruzja.pl/

Julabari | www.facebook.com/Jalabauri/

GERMANY

Arabian Harmony | www.reiterferien-bayern.eu

Goedelsteinhof | www.goedelsteinhof.de

High Pointe Tours | www.highpointetours.com/horseback-riding-vacations-germany/

Lucky Trails | www.lucky-trails.de

Old River Ranch | www.oldriverranch.de

Stone Hill Ranch | www.stone-hill-ranch.de

2019 | HORSE RIDING IN EVERY COUNTRY

GERMANY (CONTINUED)

Triple Mountain Ranch | www.triple-mountain-ranch.de

GHANA

The Green Ranch | www.greenranchlakebosomtwe.com/contactus

GREECE

Erika's Horse Farm | www.erikashorsefarm.gr

Hersonissos Horse riding | www.hersonissos-horseriding.com/romantic_moonlight.php

Ippos Molyvos

Located on a beautiful Greek Island! Tailored packages to your needs. The perfect destination to enjoy a typical sun & sea holiday in an authentic Greek village.

www.ipposmolyvos.com
ipposmolyvos@gmail.com

Kokou | www.horseridingparos.com

Odysseia Stables | www.horseriding.gr

Poseidonion Horse Riding | www.poseidonion.com/en/horse-riding

Trail Riders Corfu | www.trailriderscorfu.com

2019 | HORSE RIDING IN EVERY COUNTRY

GUATEMALA

Finca Xetuc | www.facebook.com/pg/AtFincaXetuc

Ravenscroft Riding Stables | www.ravenscroftstables.wixsite.com/

Unicornio Azul | www.unicornioazul.com/

HONDURAS

Beach Club Roatan | www.beachclubroatan.com/

Red Ridge Stables | www.redridgestable.com

HONG KONG

Hong Kong Horse Society | www.hkhorseriding.com

HUNGARY

Dirty Hooves

Ride on the ridge of the Puszta in Hungary. Wonder through forests and vineyards, gallop across hills, visit picturesque monuments and taste traditional, local cuisine and the famous Hungarian wine.

www.dirtyhooves.com
ride@dirtyhooves.com

EQUESTRIAN ADVENTURESSES

2019 | HORSE RIDING IN EVERY COUNTRY

HUNGARY (CONTINUED)

Bakodpuszta Horse Farm | www.koronatours.hu/english

Lazar Equestrian Park | www.lazarlovaspark.hu/en/

ICELAND

Hestaland | www.hestaland.net

Islenski Hesturinn | www.islenskihesturinn.is/

INDIA

Princess Trails

We are an Indo-European family company organizing horse safaris & riding holidays on well-trained Marwari horses. Small groups & family atmosphere!

www.princesstrails.com
marwarihorses@web.de

Horse India

For those with a spirit of adventure! Discover festivals, leopards, forts, palaces, the Aravalli Hills & the Great Thar Desert. Date specific group rides or 'anytime' private rides

www.horseindia.com
info@horseindia.com

2019 | HORSE RIDING IN EVERY COUNTRY

INDIA (CONTINUED)

Horse Heritage Narlai

Experience a unique stay at our rural Marwari horse farm with curly eared horses & marble columns. Ride daily & look for leopards from the terrace. Escape the chaos of India in our 5 en-suite rooms

www.horseindia.com
info@horseindia.com

Krishna Ranch | www.krishnaranch.com

Kross Terrain | www.krossterrain.com

Kutch Classic Rider Camp

The Ultimate Royal Adventure Ride.
White desert to sea on stunning Marwaris. Pristine, untouched riding terrain, superb forts & palaces, desert festivals, wildlife & culture

www.kutchclassicridercamp.com
kutchclassicridercamp@gmail.com

Mandawa Safaris | www.mandawasafaris.in

Natural Horsemanship India | www.naturalhorsemanshipindia.com

FOLLOW US & SHARE YOUR PHOTOS
@equestrianadventuresses

EQUESTRIAN ADVENTURESSES

INDONESIA

Bali Equestrian Centre | www.baliequestriancentre.com/

Kuda P Stables | www.kudapstables.com/

True Bali Experience | www.truebaliexperience.com/

Kuda P Stables | www.kudapstables.com/

Ubud Horse Stables | www.ubudhorsestables.com/index.html

IRAN

Trip to Persia | www.triptopersia.com/iran-tours/iran-horse-riding-tours

IRAQ

Erbil Horse Club | www.erbilhorseclub.com

IRELAND

Ashford Castle | www.ashfordcastle.com

Horse Holiday Farm | www.horse-holiday-farm.com

Ireland on Horseback | www.irelandonhorseback.com

2019 | HORSE RIDING IN EVERY COUNTRY

IRELAND (CONTINUED)

Lee Valley Equestrian | www.leevalleyequestriancentre.ie

ISRAEL

Sirin Riders

A rare combination of challenging rides for exp. riders, with a deep dive into the history, the archeology, & the day-to-day life of modern Israel. Together with our well-trained & happy horses, we will provide the ride of a lifetime!

www.ride-israel.com
info@ride-israel.com

EQUESTRIAN ADVENTURESSES

2019 | HORSE RIDING IN EVERY COUNTRY

ITALY

Cornacchino | www.cornacchino.it/en/start.html

EQUITANDUM

Dedicated online booking service for equestrian holidays and getaways. From weekends and holiday stays in the saddle, to multiday trails. Variety of places and regions to choose from.

www.equitandum.com
info@equitandum.com

Gelsomino Ranch | www.facebook.com/ilgelsominoranch/

Horseback.IT | www.horseback.it/index.html

JAMAICA

Half Moon | www.halfmoon.com/activities/activity/equestrian-centre/

Hooves-Guided tours on horseback | www.hooves-jamaica.com/

Reggae Horseback Riding | www.reggaehorsebackriding.com/

JAPAN

Haruka Horse Ranch | www.jphorseriding.com/

2019 | HORSE RIDING IN EVERY COUNTRY

EQUESTRIAN ADVENTURESSES
PAGE 37

2019 | HORSE RIDING IN EVERY COUNTRY

JAPAN (CONTINUED)

Horse Trekking Park | www.horsetrekking.jp/

Iejima Beachside Horse Park | www.ie-horse.wixsite.com/ieuma/english

JORDAN

Horse Riding Tours Jordan

Long canters, fast gallops, amazing scenery, great food & camping under the stars – 6-day ride.

www.horseridingtoursjordan.com
Petrabedandbreakfast@gmail.com

Jordan Desert Journeys

Adventure and retreats on Arabian Desert Horses. Max. 6-8 riders, 3-6 days, become inspired with the various tracks.

www.jordan-desert-journeys.com
info@jordan-desert-journeys.com

KAZAKHSTAN

Almaty Horse & Polo Club | www.poloclub.kz/

Astana Guide Tours | www.astanatours.kz/

2019 | HORSE RIDING IN EVERY COUNTRY

KENYA

Horse Riding in the Masai Mara

Ride w/ Elephant, buffalo, lion, & canter alongside herds of wildebeest & zebra. Led by 2 private and expert guides, 7 days, move camp 3 times. There is also plenty of opportunity to jump elephant felled logs!

https://africanhorsesafaris.com
isabel@africanhorsesafaris.com

JOIN THE COMMUNITY
facebook.com/groups/equestrianadventuresses

EQUESTRIAN ADVENTURESSES
PAGE 39

2019 | HORSE RIDING IN EVERY COUNTRY

KENYA (CONTINUED)

The Masai Mara with Gordie Church

If budget isn't a factor, then riding w/ Gordy is a privilege. Luxury service, Safari-of-a-lifetime. Ride w/ giraffe, zebra, wildebeest, lion, elephant, hippo, ostrich, warthog, leopard, cheetah – it's likely you'll see them all

https://africanhorsesafaris.com
isabel@africanhorsesafaris.com

Ol Donyo Lodge Stay

Ride along old elephant paths. The varied terrain makes for fantastic riding, trails up into the volcanic Chyulu Hills- Each ride is set to the stunning backdrop of Mt Kilimanjaro on the skyline. Luxury lodge.

https://africanhorsesafaris.com
isabel@africanhorsesafaris.com

Borana Lodge Stay

32,000 acres of unspoiled wilderness, w/ views & a new experience every day. Home to the Big 5, ride among great herds of game, admire the snow-capped peaks of Mt Kenya. Feel truly enriched. For riders and non-riders

https://africanhorsesafaris.com
isabel@africanhorsesafaris.com

Safaris Unlimited | www.safarisunlimited.com

Offbeat Safari | www.offbeatsafaris.com

2019 | HORSE RIDING IN EVERY COUNTRY

KUWAIT

Horseback Riding Kuwait | www.horsebackridingkuwait.com

Kuwait Riding Club | www.facebook.com/kuwaitrc/

KYRGYZSTAN

Mountains of Heaven

Many centuries ago the most World's famous trail – the Silk Road – ran through here. Cross snowy passes and ice-cold mountain rivers and ride in the shade of the Tian Shen, the heavenly mountains.

www.dirtyhooves.com
ride@dirtyhooves.com

Song-Kol Lake Pastures

A stunning ride through mountainous Kyrgyzstan to meet local shepherds living in their yurts at the Song-Kol lake. Enjoy the local, nomadic culture and spend nights in yurts at this marvelous lake.

www.dirtyhooves.com
ride@dirtyhooves.com

Bulak Say Horseback and Trekking | www.karakolhorsetrekking.blogspot.com/

Kyrgyz Riders Travel | www.kyrgyzriders.com/

Kyrgyz Wonders | www.facebook.com/kyrgyzwonders/

EQUESTRIAN ADVENTURESSES

2019 | HORSE RIDING IN EVERY COUNTRY

LATVIA

Adventure Ride | www.adventureride.eu/en/home

Darzini | www.facebook.com/darzinizirgi/

LEBANON

Club Hippique Libanais | www.chl-lebanon.com/6.html

Cedars Horse Riding | www.facebook.com/CedarsHorseRiding

Equestrian Circle | www.equestrian-circle.com

Lebanese Equestrian Center | www.lebaneseequestriancenter.com

LESOTHO

Drakenberg Dragons Landing | www.drakensberg.org/listing/dragons-landing/

Malealea | www.malealea.com

LIBERIA

Wulki Farms | www.facebook.com/wulkifarms/

LIBYA

Maghreb Arab Equestrian Club | www.facebook.com/MaghrebArabiEquestrianClub/

2019 | HORSE RIDING IN EVERY COUNTRY

LIECHTENSTEIN

Liechtenstein Polo Club | www.liechtensteinpolo.com/polo-club

FINLAND

Ylläksen vaellushevoset | www.yllaksenvaellushevoset.fi

MADAGASCAR

Ambaro Ranch | www.chevalnosybe.com

Faka Ranch | www.facebook.com/fakaranchfedrova/

MALAWI

Plateau Stables | www.plateaustables.com/Rates.html

MALAYSIA

Island Horses | www.langkawihorses.com/

MALTA

Golden Bay Horse Riding | www.goldenbayhorseriding.com/

Gozo Stables Horse-Riding | www.gozostables.com/

Lino's Stables | www.linostables.com/

EQUESTRIAN ADVENTURESSES

2019 | HORSE RIDING IN EVERY COUNTRY

MAURITIUS

Centre Equestre De Riambel | www.centreequestrederiambel.com/

Haras Du Morne | www.harasdumorne.com/

Maritim Equestrian Centre | www.maritimresortandspa.mu/en/activities-leisure/equestrian-centre/overview

MEXICO

Carisuva | www.ranchocarisuva.com/

Horseback Mexico | www.horsebackmexico.com/contact-us

EQUESTRIAN ADVENTURESSES
PAGE 44

2019 | HORSE RIDING IN EVERY COUNTRY

MEXICO (CONTINUED)

Leisurely Country Horseback Riding | www.horsebackridingsma.shutterfly.com/

Rancho Las Cascadas | www.rancholascascadas.com

MOLDOVA

Kskbalti | www.facebook.com/kskbalti/

Sparta Club | www.sparta-club.md

MONGOLIA

Adastra Adventure | www.adastraadventures.com

Gobi Desert Cup | www.gobidesertcup.com

Gobi Gallop | www.horsetrekmongolia.com

Imagine Riding: Mongolia 2020

Ride w/ eagle hunters in the Altai Mountains w/ pack-horses. Ride new routes through untracked wilderness and see the Sagsai Eagle festival.
2 week expedition - 2020

www.imagineriding.com
imagineriding1@gmail.com

The Adventurists - Mongol Derby | https://www.theadventurists.com/adventures/mongol-derby

Zavkhan | www.zavkhan.co.uk

2019 | HORSE RIDING IN EVERY COUNTRY

MONTENEGRO

Imagine Riding: Montenegro 2019/2020

Adventurous ride in the wild north of Montenegro where we explore new routes and few tourists are seen. Discover the breathtaking coastal mountain ranges and Montenegrin culture and hospitality.

www.imagineriding.com
imagineriding1@gmail.com

Mountain Riders | www.mountainriders.me

MOROCCO

The Berber Trail

Ride into oleander-covered valleys, see the remains of the 15th century sugarcane plantations and the Dar Caïd ruins. In the evening we'll be gazing upon the stars and singing with our Berber hosts.

www.dirtyhooves.com
ride@dirtyhooves.com

The Atlantic Coast

Gallop along the sandy beaches of the Atlantic Ocean, wade through the argan groves, enjoy the Moroccan sun and sip on wine by the bonfire light listening to the sounds of the drum in the evening.

www.dirtyhooves.com
ride@dirtyhooves.com

EQUESTRIAN ADVENTURESSES

2019 | HORSE RIDING IN EVERY COUNTRY

MOROCCO (CONTINUED)

Sahara

Follow in the footsteps of camel caravans. Cross Atlas and Anti-Atlas Mountains, rest in the date groves of the Drâa valley, meet the last nomads of Morocco and face the endless desert.

www.dirtyhooves.com
ride@dirtyhooves.com

Amodou Cheval | www.amodoucheval.com/

Equi Evasion | www.equievasion.com

Morocco Sahara to Atlantic Long Ride : February 2020

We are planning a 900 km ride from the edge of the Sahara to the Atlantic on magnificent Arab-Berber stallions! Join for 2 weeks or the full ride.

www.imagineriding.com
imagineriding1@gmail.com

Ranch Les 2 Gazelles

We welcome you all year. With beach, mountain and desert trails you will discover authentic landscapes. Enjoy the comfort of typical accommodations and flavors of Moroccan food!

www.les2gazelles.com/en/
les2gazelles@gmail.com

EQUESTRIAN ADVENTURESSES

2019 | HORSE RIDING IN EVERY COUNTRY

MOROCCO (CONTINUED)

Zouina Cheval

Trails in countryside & beaches w/ nights in camp
English speaking guides. Run all year round.
Group size 2-12 persons

www.zouina-cheval.com
contact@zouina-cheval.com

MOZAMBIQUE

Surf and Turf Horse Safari

For those who love the exotic, post-card perfect paradise. Thrilling beach canters & horse swims. Beautiful coastal lodge, which boasts stunning views out across Bazaruto Archipelago bay.

https://africanhorsesafaris.com
isabel@africanhorsesafaris.com

Mozambique Horse Safari | www.mozambiquehorsesafari.com

MYANMAR

Ayeindamar tour | www.ayeindamartour.com

Inle Horse Club | www.inlehorseclub.com

2019 | HORSE RIDING IN EVERY COUNTRY
NAMIBIA

Namib Desert Horse Safari

Ride across the Namib Desert. Tackle this challenge aboard super fit, & sure-footed horses. Some great 'let the dogs loose' gallops. Not for the faint-hearted, 350km adventure across 10 days.

https://africanhorsesafaris.com
isabel@africanhorsesafaris.com

Damaraland Ride

Virtually inaccessible, Ancient craters and prehistoric remnants dot the distant horizons. Skeleton Coast w/ its museum of shipwrecks – a journey you will never forget. Exp. Riders ONLY

https://africanhorsesafaris.com
isabel@africanhorsesafaris.com

Equitrails Namibia | www.equitrails.org

Gross Okandjou | www.gross-okandjou.de/

Okakambe Trails | www.okakambe.iway.na/

Okapuka Horse Safaris | www.okapuka.com

NEPAL

Gokarna Forest Resort | www.gokarna.com/horse-ride

2019 | HORSE RIDING IN EVERY COUNTRY

NETHERLANDS

De boschhoeve | www.de-boschhoeve.nl

Pur Terschelling | www.puur-terschelling.nl

Rijstal De Blinkert | www.rijstaldeblinkert.nl/rijstal-de-blinkert/

NEW ZEALAND

Adventure Horse Trekking | www.adventurehorsetrekking.co.nz

High Country Horses | www.highcountryhorses.nz

Horse Trekking Lake Okareka | www.treklakeokareka.co.nz

Ngatuna Backpackers | www.facebook.com/ngatunabackpackers/

The Cardrona | www.thecardrona.co.nz

NICARAGUA

Haris'horses | www.harishorsesnicaragua.com

Rancho Chilamate Adventures on Horseback | www.ranchochilamate.com

JOIN THE COMMUNITY
facebook.com/groups/equestrianadventuresses

2019 | HORSE RIDING IN EVERY COUNTRY

NIGER

Club Equestre De Niamey | www.clubequestredeniamey.blogspot.com

NIGERIA

Lagos Polo Club | www.lagospolo.com

NORWAY

Gullverkstallen | www.gullverkstallen.no/

Hov Gard | www.hovgard.no/en/

Mesna Activities & Accommodation | www.mesna.no

OMAN

Oman Horse Riding Holidays | www.oman-horseridingholidays.com

PANAMA

Bluff Beach Retreat Horseback Riding | www.bluffbeachretreat.com/horseback-riding-in-bocas-del-toro/

Junglecat Panama | www.facebook.com/junglecatpanama

PAPUA NEW GUINEA

Koitaki Country Club | www.papuanewguinea.travel/koitaki-country-club

2019 | HORSE RIDING IN EVERY COUNTRY

PARAGUAY

Cabana Austria | www.cabana-austria.com/en/activities/

South America Inside | www.southamerica-inside.com/en/farm-stay-projects/farm-stay-paraguay-en

Trico Tours | www.tricotours.com/day-tours-circuito-de-oro/ranch-experience/

PERU

Dirty Hooves

An amazing adventure in Peru with the local Paso Peruano horses, famous for their smooth walk. Ride towards the slopes of Andes, covered with jungle, right into the The Sacred Valley of the Incas.

www.dirtyhooves.com
ride@dirtyhooves.com

Cusco for You Salineras Ranch | www.cuscoforyou.com

Hacienda del Chalán

On the smoothest Paso Horses through the Peruvian Andes. Amazing nature and Inca culture. 2-6 days tours.

www.haciendadelchalan.com
reservas@haciendadelchalan.com

Horseback Riding Cusco-Day tours | www.horsebackridingcusco.com

2019 | HORSE RIDING IN EVERY COUNTRY

PHILIPPINES

Boracay Horse Riding Stables | www.myboracayguide.com/boracay-activities/horse-riding/

El Kabayo Stables | www.elkabayostables.com

Happy Horse Farms Equestrian Center | www.hhfequestrian.com/

POLAND

EQUITANDUM

Dedicated online booking service for equestrian holidays and getaways. From weekends and holiday stays in the saddle, to multiday trails. Variety of places and regions to choose from.

www.equitandum.com
info@equitandum.com

PORTUGAL

Equo Resort | www.montevelho.pt

Lusitano Trail Rides | www.lusitanotrailrides.jimdo.com

Quintadasaudade | www.quintadasaudade.com

QATAR

Al Shaqab | www.alshaqab.com

2019 | HORSE RIDING IN EVERY COUNTRY

REPUBLIC OF KOREA

Package Korea | www.packagekorea.com/tour/horse-riding-tour/

Horseland Jeju | www.jejuhorse.com

ROMANIA

Dirty Hooves

Transylvania, the land of Dracula and beautiful, wild mountains. Untouched nature of the southern Carpathians, charming valleys, medieval villages and natural, local food make it a very pleasant ride.

www.dirtyhooves.com
ride@dirtyhooves.com

 Cross country farm | www.cross-country.ro

Husar Riding Centre | www.english.husarslanic.com/

Icelandic Horses Riding Ranch | www.izlandilovak.ro

Imagine Riding: Transylvania 2019/2020

One of the most unspoiled regions in Europe; a land w/ ancient forests, rich traditions, & no fences. Go back in time! Experience w/ locals who are excellent horsemen & grew up in these villages.

www.imagineriding.com
imagineriding1@gmail.com

2019 | HORSE RIDING IN EVERY COUNTRY

ROMANIA (CONTINUED)

Spiritul Cailor | www.echitatiespiritulcailor.wordpress.com/

RUSSIAN FEDERATION

Cossack Horse Riding Club | www.horse-kmv.ru/

RWANDA

Fazenda Sengha | www.sengha.com/

SAN MARINO

Centro Equestre Valgiurata | www.centroequestrevalgiurata.blogspot.com

SAUDI ARABIA

Dirab Golf Club | www.dirabgolf.com

Equestrian Club of Riyadh | www.frusiya.com/

SENEGAL

Horses of the Sea | www.espritdafrique-senegal.com/chevaux-du-lac

FOLLOW US & SHARE YOUR PHOTOS

@equestrianadventuresses

SERBIA

Equestrian Adventure Serbia | www.equestrianadventure-serbia.org/

Equestrian Club Kentaur | www.kentaur.club/

Konjicki klub Arandelovac | www.konjickiklubarandjelovac.rs/sr-yu/

SEYCHELLES

Turquoise Horse Trails | www.turquoisehorsetrails.com/

SINGAPORE

Bukit Timah Saddle Club | http://www.btsc.org.sg

Singapore Polo Club | www.singaporepoloclub.org/

SLOVAKIA

Travel Slovakia | www.travelslovakia.sk/slovakia-trips/agrotourism-slovakia/horse-riding-high-tatras.php

SLOVENIA

Farm at Kolenc | www.facebook.com/kmetijakolenc/

Horses on Breg | www.konji-na-bregu.business.site

Mrcina Ranch | www.ranc-mrcina.com/

2019 | HORSE RIDING IN EVERY COUNTRY

SLOVENIA (CONTINUED)

Pristava Lepena | www.en.pristava-lepena.com/horseback-riding

Slovenia Horse Riding | www.sloveniahorseriding.com/

SOUTH AFRICA

Big 5 Horse Safari

Big 5 Game Reserve. Exhilarating - fast-paced, exciting from start to end, w/ incredible close encounters. Luxury tents 4 nights, alfresco dining, lodge w/ infinity pool over-looking watering hole for 2 nights

https://africanhorsesafaris.com
isabel@africanhorsesafaris.com

EquestrianAdventuresses.com

Get your Equestrian Adventuresses T-Shirts and Hoodies!

EQUESTRIAN ADVENTURESSES

2019 | HORSE RIDING IN EVERY COUNTRY

SOUTH AFRICA (CONTINUED)

Wild Coast Horse Safari

Pristine beaches. Experience the freedom of coastal riding - fulfill every rider's dream; cantering down vast empty beaches – bliss. Led by 2 competitive endurance riders, who keep the horses super fit, & the pace upbeat!

https://africanhorsesafaris.com
isabel@africanhorsesafaris.com

Working-Holiday Program

If you're looking to gain exp riding & volunteering w/ horses, while embracing everything the bush has to offer, then this is for you. Unbeatable riding experiences, & spend time in the bush, acquiring knowledge.

https://africanhorsesafaris.com
isabel@africanhorsesafaris.com

Riding at Ants Hill & Ants Nest

Excellent riding, excellent horses & variety of game including, giraffe, rhino, buffalo, zebra & antelope. Lodge based - All riding abilities welcome -no lions or elephants in the reserve. Non-riding activities

https://africanhorsesafaris.com
isabel@africanhorsesafaris.com

2019 | HORSE RIDING IN EVERY COUNTRY

SOUTH AFRICA (CONTINUED)

Riding in the Cape Winelands

Wining & dining! Splendid mountains, lush vineyards, Dutch homesteads, steeped in history. Spend the mornings on horseback & be met by delicious wine tastings & fine cuisine. Remount, & enjoy afternoon ride.

https://africanhorsesafaris.com
isabel@africanhorsesafaris.com

Addo Elephant National Park Horse Trails | www.facebook.com/Addo-Elephant-National-Park-Horse-Trails

Africa Conservation Experience - Unique Horseback Safari

Do you want to see wildlife conservation from a new perspective? Would you like to combine your love of horse riding with the chance to protect Africa's wildlife? Then this is the experience for you.

www.conservationafrica.net
info@conservationafrica.net

Africa Dream Horse Safari | www.africandreamhorsesafari.co.za

Black Horse Trails | www.blackhorsetrails.co.za/

Heaven and Earth Trails | www.heavenandearthtrails.co.za/

Holistic Horse Farm | www.holistic-horse-paddock-paradise.business.site

2019 | HORSE RIDING IN EVERY COUNTRY

SOUTH AFRICA (CONTINUED)

Horse About Trails | www.horseabout.co.za

Horizon Horseback | www.ridinginafrica.com

Khotso | www.khotso.co.za

Moolmanshoek | www.moolmanshoek.co.za

Wild Coast Horseback Adventures | www.wildcoasthorsebackadventures.com

SPAIN

Horse Riding Holidays Andalucia | www.horseriding-holidays-andalucia.com/

Imagine Riding: Transhumance Ride 2019/2020

Time travel along the Cañadas Reales: the ancient Transhumance cattle route taken twice a year, from summer pastures in the Mountains to the winter pastures in Extremadura.

www.imagineriding.com
imagineriding1@gmail.com

Jerebeque Trails Horse Riding Holidays | www.ridingholidaysspain.com

Los Alamos | www.losalamosriding.co.uk

Panorama Trails | www.panorama-trails.com/en/

2019 | HORSE RIDING IN EVERY COUNTRY

SPAIN (CONTINUED)

Ride Andalucia | www.rideandalucia.net

SIERRA TRAILS – MOUNTAIN WILDERNESS TRAILS– ANDALUCIA – SPAIN
Explore this unique region with beautiful Spanish horses. Fully inclusive 7 day treks and 3 day short breaks. Move nightly from charming mountain village to village. Group Sizes 4 – 10, March – Nov
www.spain-horse-riding.com
dallas@spainhorseriding.com

SRI LANKA

Ceylon Riding club | www.ceylonridingclub.com

Forest Park | www.forestpark.lk

ST. KITTS & NEVIS

Nevis Equestrian Centre | www.nevishorseback.com

ST. LUCIA

Atlantic Shores Riding Stables | www.atlanticridingstables.com

East Coast Riding Stable | www.eastcoaststable.com

Holiday Riding Stable | www.holidayridingstablesstlucia.weebly.com/

2019 | HORSE RIDING IN EVERY COUNTRY

ST. VINCENT & GRENADINES

Mustique Island | www.mustique-island.com/activities/equestrian/

SURINAME

Club Neutraal | www.facebook.com/clubneutraal/

Manege Ponderosa | www.facebook.com/pages/category/Stadium--Arena---Sports-Venue/Manege-Ponderosa

Rimboe | www.facebook.com/Rimboe-horse-World-Suriname-353037708201515/

SWAZILAND

Mlolwane Wild Sanctuary | www.biggameparks.org/properties/mlilwane-wildlife-sanctuary-2

SWEDEN

Horses of Taiga | www.horsesoftaiga.com

Ofelas Icelandic horses & Guide Service | www.ofelas.se/en/home/

Our Little Farm | www.ourlittlefarm.se

FOLLOW US & SHARE YOUR PHOTOS
@equestrianadventuresses

EQUESTRIAN ADVENTURESSES

2019 | HORSE RIDING IN EVERY COUNTRY

SWITZERLAND

Engadin River Ranch | www.engadin-riverranch.ch/index.php/de/

Ginas Reitschule | www.engadin-reiten.ch

Leventinawestern | www.leventinawestern.ch/

THAILAND

Phuket International Horse Club | www.phukethorseclub.com/

Phuket Riding Club | www.phuketridingclub.com/

Thai Horse Farm | www.daytripchiangmai.com

THE REPUBLIC OF NORTH MACEDONIA

SHERPA HORSE RIDING

Experience epic horse riding adventures and the unique beauty of Macedonian's mountains.
THE MIYAK'S TRIBE TRAILS 7 overnights, 6 days riding- All inclusive
May till November Size 2-10 Persons

www.horseriding.com.mk
hcbistragalicnik@gmail.com

FOLLOW US & SHARE YOUR PHOTOS

  @equestrianadventuresses

EQUESTRIAN ADVENTURESSES

2019 | HORSE RIDING IN EVERY COUNTRY

JOIN THE COMMUNITY
facebook.com/groups/equestrianadventuresses

THE REPUBLIC OF NORTH MACEDONIA (CONTINUED)

SHERPA HORSE RIDING

THE BUCEPHALUS TRAILS 5 overnight 4 days riding - All inclusive
May till November Size 2-10 Persons

www.horseriding.com.mk
hcbistragalicnik@gmail.com

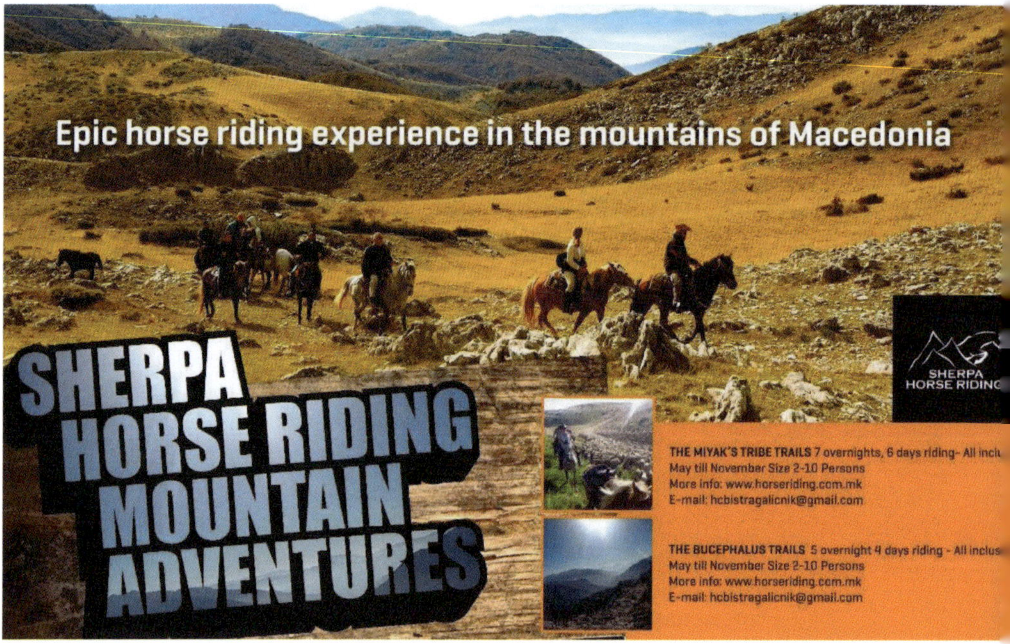

TRINIDAD AND TOBAGO

Being with Horses | www.being-with-horses.com/

Friendship Riding Stables | www.friendshipridingstables.com/#!

Saddle Valley Stables | www.facebook.com/SaddleValleyStables/

TUNISIA

Mezraya Ranch | www.mezrayaranch.com/fr/a-propos-de/

Ranch Tanit Djerba | www.ranch-tanit-djerba.com/?lang=en

Ranch Yassmina Djerba La Douce | www.ranchyassmina.wixsite.com/home

TURKEY

Akhal Teke Horse Center | www.akhal-tekehorsecenter.com

Cemal Ranch | www.cemalranch.com/

Moonlight Horse Ranch | www.moonlighthorseranch.com/

The Dalton Brothers Ranch | www.cappadociahorseriding.com/

TURKMENISTAN

Ayan Travel | www.ayan-travel.com

2019 | HORSE RIDING IN EVERY COUNTRY

TURKS & CAICOS

Provo Ponies | www.provoponies.com

UGANDA

GreenGo Horse Farm | www.greengo-equestrian-club.business.site

Nile Horseback Safaris | www.nilehorsebacksafaris.com/nile_horseback_safaris_about_us.asp

UKRAINE

Dirty Hooves

Ride through endless plains, vast fields and forests of wester Ukraine, bath in rivers and pass through small villages. Historical Podolia is where East meets West and time passes by at a slower pace.

www.dirtyhooves.com
ride@dirtyhooves.com

Idilliya Stable | www.idyllium.wixsite.com/alba

Stetson Equestrian Club | www.stetson.com.ua/

UNITED ARAB EMIRATES

Al Jiyad Stables | www.aljiyadstables.com/

EQUESTRIAN ADVENTURESSES

2019 | HORSE RIDING IN EVERY COUNTRY
UNITED ARAB EMIRATES (CONTINUED)

Dhabian Equestrian Center | www.dhabianequi.com

Dubai Desert Horse Ride Experience | www.ddhre.webs.com/

Winners Equestrian Club | www.winnersequestrian.com/

UNITED KINGDOM

Adventure Clydesdale | www.adventureclydesdale.com

Cumbrian Heavy Horses | www.cumbrianheavyhorses.com

Liberty Trails | www.liberty-trails.com

Peers Clough Pack Horses | www.peerscloughpackhorses.co.uk

Tally Ho Stables | www.tallyhostables.co.uk/

The Friesian Experience | www.thefriesianexperience.org

ISLE OF WIGHT

Island Riding | www.islandriding.com/riding-holidays/

SCOTLAND

Highlands Unbridled | www.highlandsunbridled.com

2019 | HORSE RIDING IN EVERY COUNTRY

UNITED KINGDOM (CONTINUED)

Lochness Riding | www.lochnessriding.co.uk

Wilder Ways | www.wilderways.scot

WALES

Trans Wales Horseback Trails | www.transwales.com

UNITED REPUBLIC OF TANZANIA

Mt Kilimanjaro Elephant Ride

Follow in the footsteps of elephants. Trail riding, mobile camp, 7 nights watching sunsets, sitting round campfires & sleeping out in the wilderness. An adventure like no other!

https://africanhorsesafaris.com
isabel@africanhorsesafaris.com

Maisha Mazuri Horse Riding Club | www.facebook.com/MaishaMazuriHorseRidingClub

Zanzibar Horse Club | www.zanzibarhorseclub.com/

FOLLOW US & SHARE YOUR PHOTOS

@equestrianadventuresses

2019 | HORSE RIDING IN EVERY COUNTRY

UNITED STATES
COLORADO

Cherokee Park Ranch

Voted USA's #1 Dude Ranch! Talented horses + breathtaking scenery + delicious food + incredible people + endless fun!

www.cherokeeparkranch.com
info@cherokeeparkranch.com

Zapata Ranch | www.zranch.org

ARIZONA

Boyd Ranch Mule Ride | www.boydranch.org/boyd-ranch-mule-ride/

Hacienda Del Sol | www.haciendadelsol.com

FLORIDA

Tropical Trail Rides | www.tropicaltrailrides.com

MONTANA

Swan Mountain Outfitters | www.swanmountainoutfitters.com

*LOOK OUT FOR OUR UPCOMING CATALOG: "HORSE RIDING IN EVERY STATE IN THE USA" FOR MORE LOCATIONS!

EQUESTRIAN ADVENTURESSES

2019 | HORSE RIDING IN EVERY COUNTRY

VANUATU

Bellevue Ranch | www.bellevueranchvanuatu.com/

Club Hippique Adventure Park | www.club-hippique-horse-riding.squarespace.com/

Santo Horse Adventures | www.facebook.com/pg/SantoHorseAdventures/about/

VENEZUELA

Hacienda Macanao | www.haciendamacanao.com/

Ranch Cabatucan | www.cabatucan.com/

VIETNAM

Ngua Hanoi Horse Club | www.nguahanoi.vn

ZAMBIA

Ride Zambezi Private Trails | www.ridezambezi.com/#

EQUESTRIAN ADVENTURESSES

2019 | HORSE RIDING IN EVERY COUNTRY

ZIMBABWE

Zimbabwe Working-Holiday Programme

Receive hands-on experience, help manage the stables, try your hand at basic vet tasks, take out safari rides, lessons, carriage safaris in the African bush. Ride alongside plains game, swim w/ horses, learn to play polocrosse etc

https://africanhorsesafaris.com
isabel@africanhorsesafaris.com

Zambezi Horse Safari – Victoria Falls

Follow the footsteps of David Livingstone; ride near the magnificent Zambezi River. Variety of landscapes; catch panoramic views, gain insights to rural African life, canter across grassy plains & spot game. Stay in 2 special locations

https://africanhorsesafaris.com
isabel@africanhorsesafaris.com

Ride Zimbabwe

Explore the most pristine & remote areas of Zimbabwe while rhino tracking on horseback, riding alongside magnificent herds of Sable & getting up close to magnificent elephant herds!

https://ridezimbabwe.com/
admin@vardensafaris.com

Zambezi Horse Trails | www.zambezihorsetrails.com

EQUESTRIAN ADVENTURESSES

2019 | HORSE RIDING IN EVERY COUNTRY

2019/2020 EDITION

WWW.EQUESTRIANADVENTURESSES.COM

FACEBOOK GROUP:
WWW.FACEBOOK.COM/GROUPS/EQUESTRIAN ADVENTURESSES

INSTAGRAM:
@EQUESTRIANADVENTURESSES

EQUESTRIAN ADVENTURESSES

Printed in Dunstable, United Kingdom